Ocean Explorers

Contents

The World Unknown 4

The Viking Explorers 6

The Island Adventurers 8

Land Ahoy! 10

Galleons of Gold 12

Tall Tales 14

Icebreakers 16

Sailing the High Seas 18

A Spirit of Adventure 20

Glossary 22

Index 23

Discussion Starters 24

Features

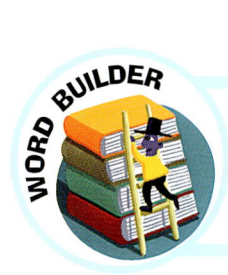

WORD BUILDER

The Vikings were sailors from long ago. They lived in northern Europe. Turn to page 7 to learn what the word *Viking* really means.

TIME LINK

When did people first discover and settle islands in the Pacific Ocean? Turn to page 8 to learn about these amazing adventurers.

TECHTALK

How can a captain know exactly where a ship is at sea? Find out how technology helps ocean explorers on page 18.

PROFILE

An adventurous teenager recently became the youngest person to sail alone around the world. Read **A Spirit of Adventure** on page 20 to find out who he is.

SITESEEING · PAST & FUTURE

Learn how to build your own model ship.
Visit **www.infosteps.co.uk**
for more about **SHIPS AND SAILING**.

The World Unknown

The ocean is a place of adventure and discovery. For many years explorers have sailed across wild seas in search of new lands.

They set sail in many kinds of ships. They didn't always know where their journey would take them. They returned with new knowledge that helped build a better picture of the world. Slowly the mapping of Earth's real land and sea began to take shape.

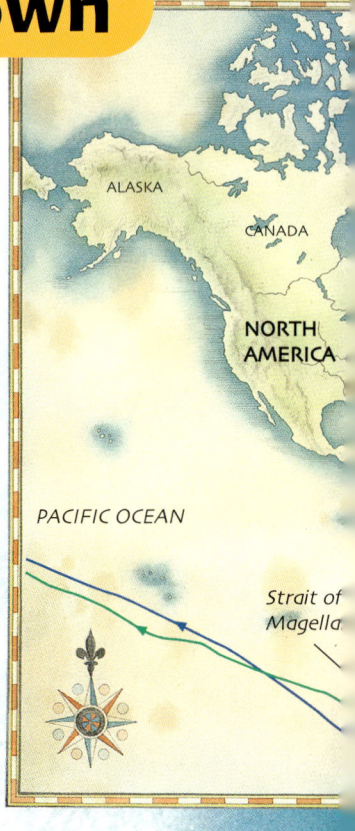

Viking longship

Polynesian canoe

Mapmakers, or **cartographers**, have made a better picture of the world with each new voyage and discovery.

KEY		
	Explorer	Year
—	Leif Erikson	1000–1001
—	Christopher Columbus First voyage	1492–1493
- - -	Fourth voyage	1502–1504
—	Voyage begun by Ferdinand Magellan	1519–1522
—	Henry Hudson	1610
—	Abel Tasman	1642–1644
—	James Cook's first voyage	1768–1771

Chinese junk

Clipper

5

The Viking Explorers

Viking sailors from Sweden, Denmark and Norway were among the earliest ocean explorers. The Vikings were good sailors and shipbuilders. They made strong fast ships from wood. They loaded their ships with **cargo** such as furs to trade and set off, hoping to discover more land.

Many people were afraid of these Viking warriors who sailed the wild and stormy seas with ease.

A famous Viking explorer named Leif Erikson was the first person from Europe to land in North America. He landed over 1,000 years ago.

GREENLAND
ICELAND
VINLAND
FAEROE ISLANDS
NORWAY
SWEDEN
DENMARK
Baltic Sea
Dnieper River
Volga River
Kiev
Caspian Sea
NORMANDY
Black Sea
Luna
SPAIN
Seville
Miklagård (Constantinople)
To Baghdad
Mediterranean Sea

WORD BUILDER

The Vikings invaded many of the lands they discovered. The word *Viking* comes from a Norse word meaning "piracy".

The Island Adventurers

While the Vikings explored northern seas, people from Polynesia were exploring the huge Pacific Ocean. With their families, they paddled across the sea in long strong canoes full of **produce** such as bananas and coconuts. These sailors had nothing to guide them but the patterns of the stars and the rhythms of the ocean currents. They discovered and settled many new lands.

Year 400
People from Polynesia settle Easter Island in the Pacific.

Year 600
Polynesians settle the Hawaiian islands.

Year 750
Polynesians arrive in New Zealand.

WORD BUILDER

This southern part of the world is now called *Polynesia*. The name Polynesia means "many islands".

1642
Ocean explorer Abel Tasman from Europe arrives in New Zealand.

1779
Captain James Cook reaches Hawaii.

9

Land Ahoy!

Land was a welcome sight for men and women who had been at sea for months at a time. One of the longest sea voyages was in 1492 when the explorer Christopher Columbus sailed west from Spain with a **fleet** of ships. Columbus reached a great and rich land area— the Americas. He thought he had found Asia, but he landed in what was soon called the New World.

The *Santa Maria,* shown here, was Columbus' special **flagship**.

1 Crow's-nest
2 Captain's cabin
3 Upper deck
4 Food stores

New World | Spain
ATLANTIC OCEAN

Columbus crossed the stormy Atlantic Ocean four times.

11

Galleons of Gold

The Spanish set sail for the rich New World early in the 1500s. They crossed the ocean in great ships called **galleons**. They were greedy for the treasures of the New World, so they filled their ships with gold and jewels from the areas of Mexico and Peru.

Pirates often attacked the galleons to take their treasure. The seas became dangerous with the criss-crossing of ships and swords. But from this time on people began to sail to all parts of the world.

1519

A famous explorer from Portugal named Ferdinand Magellan was the first person to lead a voyage around the world. His journey proved once and for all that Earth is round.

Tall Tales

Sailors saw many surprising sights during their travels. They also faced many dangers. Sometimes danger came as a mighty storm, jagged rocks or high seas. Sometimes it was the mystery and fear of the unknown. Sailors often told tales of terrible sea monsters, singing mermaids and wicked pirates. As they travelled from port to port the stories grew beyond the truth to become larger than life.

WORD BUILDER

Pirates began attacking and robbing ships in very early times. Some pirates of the past, such as Blackbeard, became so famous that they live on today as **legends**. Stories about pirates are still popular. They sometimes give the wrong idea that pirates lived only in the past. In fact pirates still rob ships in parts of the world today. The word pirate means "sea robber".

SITESEEING · PAST & FUTURE

Learn how to build your own model ship.
Visit www.infosteps.co.uk
for more about SHIPS AND SAILING.

Icebreakers

The icy waters of the North Atlantic Ocean were the most dangerous parts of the world for early ocean explorers. Here sailors saw icebergs as big as skyscrapers. They had to **navigate** through freezing waters of jagged ice. Sometimes ships were trapped in the ice for months. The crew would run out of fresh food and become ill with a disease called **scurvy**.

Special ships called icebreakers are used today to make passages through thick ice for other ships.

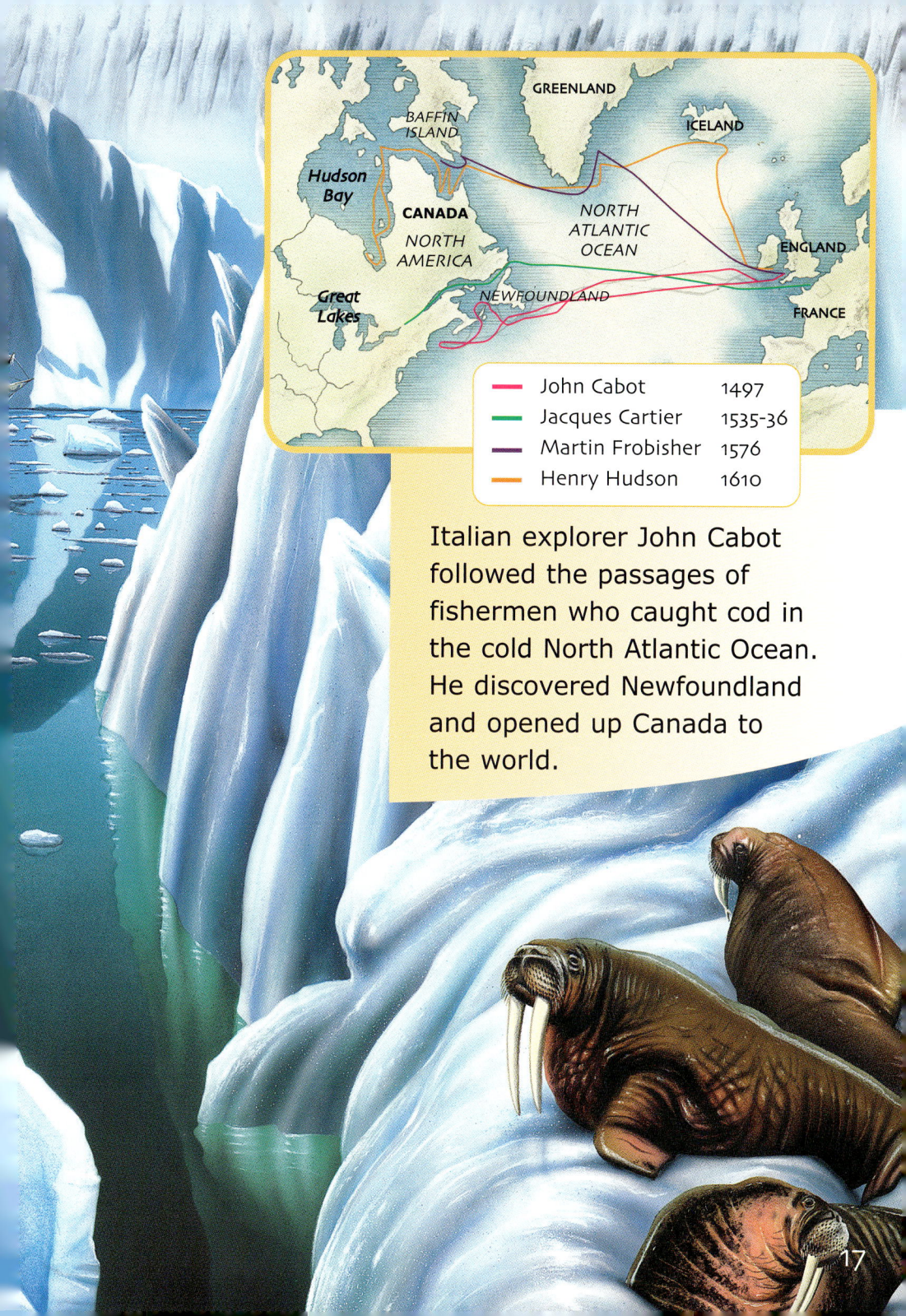

	John Cabot	1497
	Jacques Cartier	1535-36
	Martin Frobisher	1576
	Henry Hudson	1610

Italian explorer John Cabot followed the passages of fishermen who caught cod in the cold North Atlantic Ocean. He discovered Newfoundland and opened up Canada to the world.

Sailing the High Seas

Today ships of all shapes and sizes cross the world's oceans. Container ships carry cargo around the world. Huge cruise ships carry people to many countries. There are fishing boats, sailing boats, racing boats and rescue boats. The captains of these vessels do not have to navigate by the stars. High-tech tools tell them where they are and help to keep them going in the right direction.

TECHTALK

It once took great time and effort for early explorers to figure out where they were at sea. Today, a satellite computer system called The Global Positioning System (G.P.S.) displays a ship's position when the captain presses a button.

Container ship

Rescue boat

Fishing boat

Receiver

Satellite

G.P.S. display monitor

19

PROFILE

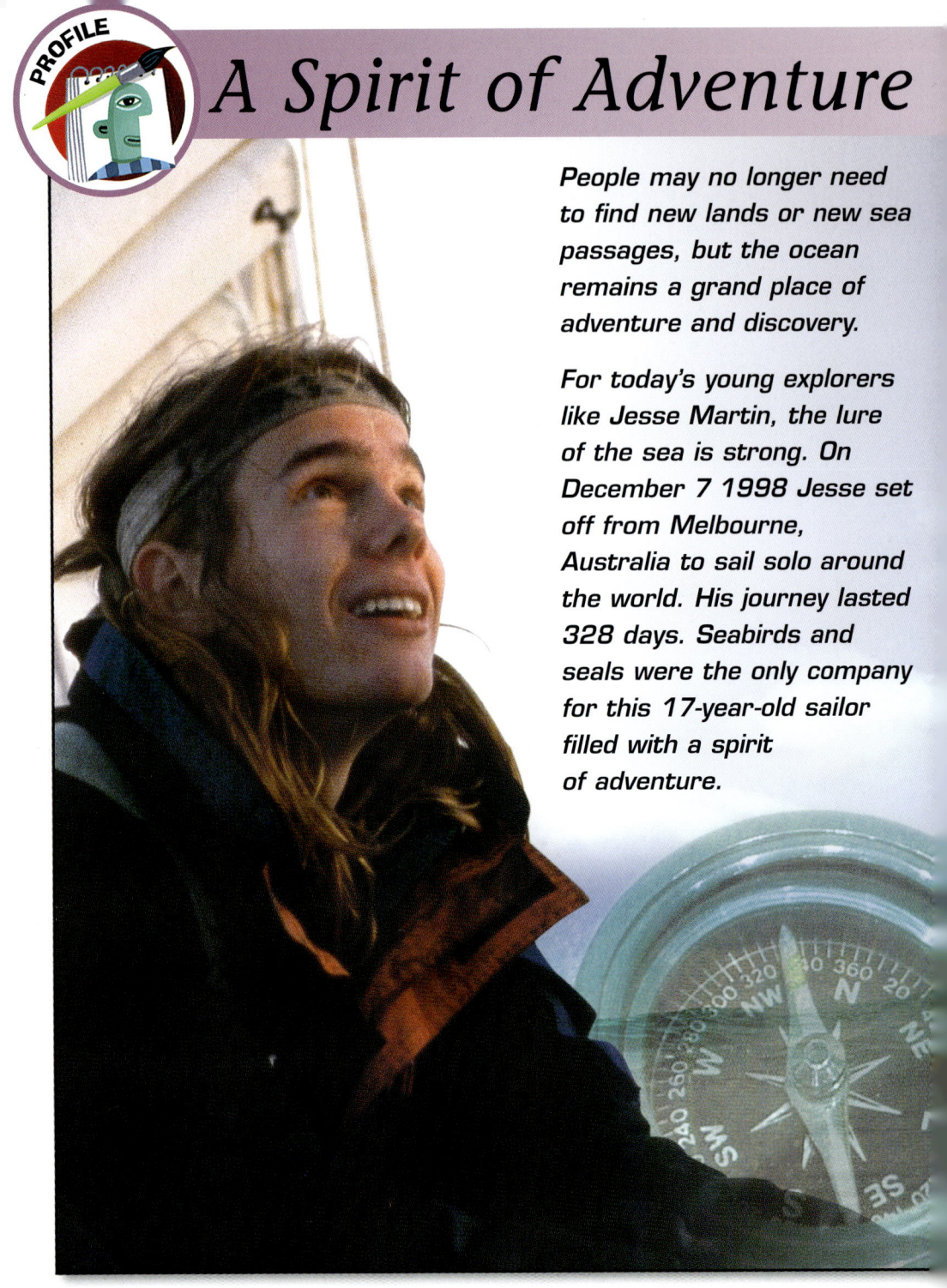

A Spirit of Adventure

People may no longer need to find new lands or new sea passages, but the ocean remains a grand place of adventure and discovery.

For today's young explorers like Jesse Martin, the lure of the sea is strong. On December 7 1998 Jesse set off from Melbourne, Australia to sail solo around the world. His journey lasted 328 days. Seabirds and seals were the only company for this 17-year-old sailor filled with a spirit of adventure.

Map of Jesse's Journey

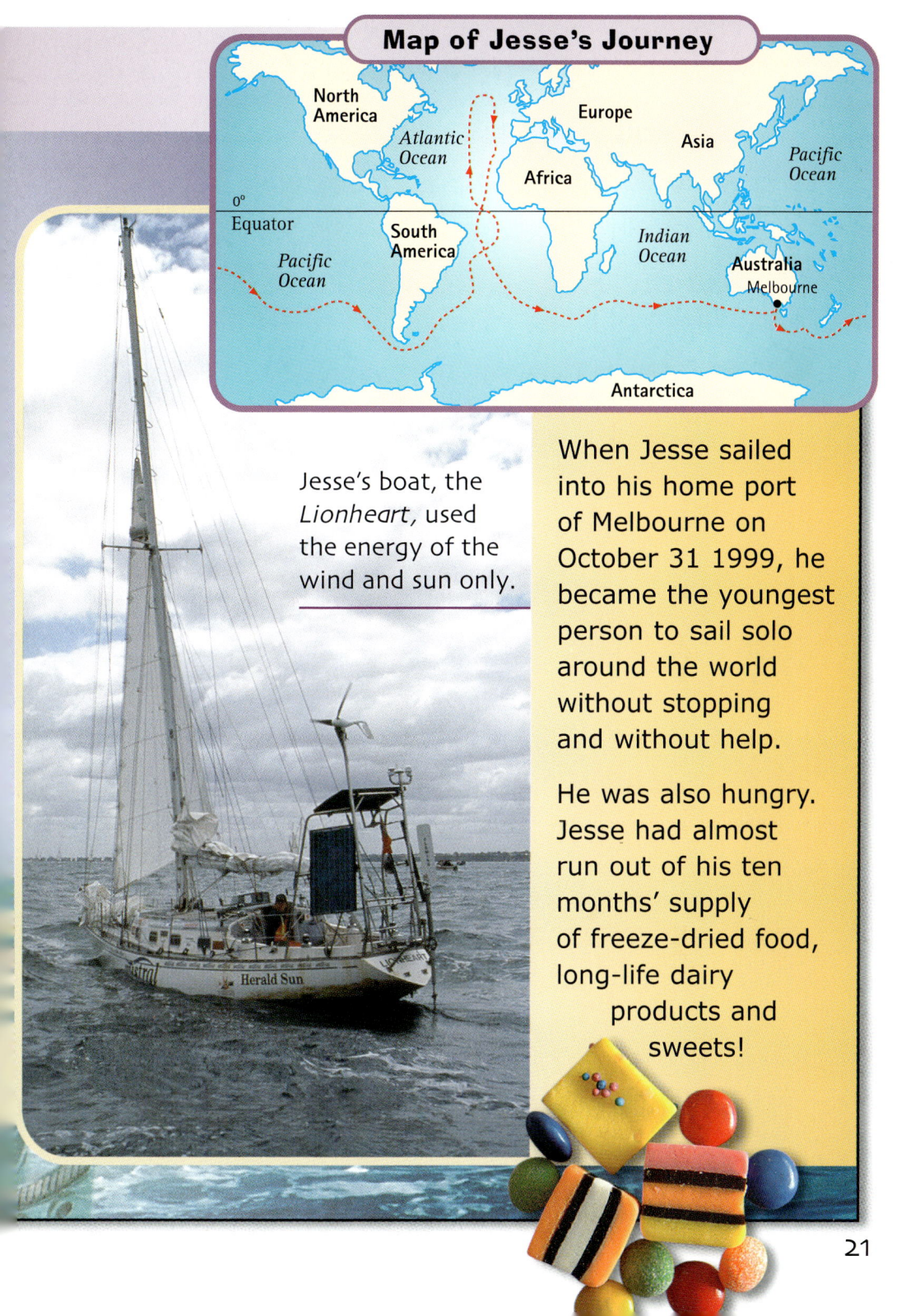

Jesse's boat, the *Lionheart,* used the energy of the wind and sun only.

When Jesse sailed into his home port of Melbourne on October 31 1999, he became the youngest person to sail solo around the world without stopping and without help.

He was also hungry. Jesse had almost run out of his ten months' supply of freeze-dried food, long-life dairy products and sweets!

21

Glossary

cargo – the load that a ship carries. Ships carry cargo such as food and cars.

cartographer – a person who makes maps. Cartographers use lines, colours, shapes and symbols to design maps.

flagship – a ship that carries the leader of a fleet of ships. A flagship flies a special flag to show that person is on board.

fleet – a group of ships travelling together and all under the control of one leader

galleon – a heavy wooden sailing ship with square sails used long ago

legend – an old story based on something real but changed so all of it is no longer true

navigate – to steer a ship or boat and find a way across water

produce – fresh fruit and vegetables

scurvy – a disease that early sailors often suffered on long sea voyages. Scurvy is caused by a lack of Vitamin C, which is in fresh fruit and vegetables.

Index

Cabot, John   17

cargo   6, 18

cartographers   5

Columbus, Christopher   5, 10–11

Cook, Captain James   5, 9

Erikson, Leif   5–6

G.P.S.   18–19

Hudson, Henry   5, 17

Magellan, Ferdinand   5, 13

maps   4–5, 7, 9, 11, 17, 21

Martin, Jesse   20–21

pirates   12, 14–15

Polynesia   4, 8–9

scurvy   16

ships   4–6, 10, 12, 15–16, 18–19

Tasman, Abel   5, 9

treasure   12

Vikings   4, 6–8

23

Discussion Starters

1 If someone is going to sail the world alone, what planning would need to be done ahead of time? What should be taken along? Why?

2 If you had been at sea for months and months and at long last stepped onto dry land, what is the first thing you would do? What would you have missed most about the land?

3 Explorers have now discovered and mapped most of Earth. Where might there still be hidden and unknown lands to explore? What do you think they might be like?